STYLE ICONS

HELEN GREEN & ELIZABETH WEITZMAN

AND THE BEAT GOES ON.

Beat

CHER: SHAPE SHIFTER AND SURVIVOR

If we could turn back time – all the way to 1962 – we'd find a sixteen-year-old runaway, a scared high-school dropout in threadbare thrift, sitting in an LA coffee shop wondering where to go and what to do next. Cherilyn Sarkisian had little support, and no direction, when a twenty-seven-year-old record company assistant named Salvatore Bono walked in and sat down at her table. He brought her up to the studio where he worked, and the legendary (and now notorious) record producer Phil Spector soon signed her up for her first gig, as a backup singer for Darlene Love.

She was a survivor already, and the strength she developed in her early years has served her ever since. As she herself has said, "It wasn't pretty, and it was never easy."

Cher was born in 1946 to a teenage single mother named Jackie Jean – an impoverished but talented singer who changed her name to Georgia, entered beauty pageants, and aimed for Hollywood stardom. Georgia's unrealized dreams eventually landed on her eldest daughter, a natural rebel whose own striking beauty happened to be dramatically out of step with the times.

And there lies the secret of Cher: she's never much cared about trends, or styles, or other people's opinions. She's always done whatever feels right to her – in her career, in fashion, in life – and allowed the world to follow.

The Free Spirit, the Warrior Goddess, the Disco Diva, and the Comeback Queen: these weren't faddish phases, or calculated reinventions. She envisioned them – usually alongside celebrated designer Bob Mackie – as embodiments of self-expression, a way to speak to ... well, whoever needed to hear. Kids who felt out of synch in a conformist society. Critics who snubbed her talents because they didn't like her look. Media that wrote her off for being too odd, too old, *too much.*

Her lifelong rejection of sexism, ageism, homophobia, and rigid conventionality – often articulated through fashion itself – has inspired artists like Madonna, Lady Gaga, Cardi B, and Beyoncé.

And she *still* hasn't stopped rewriting the rules. A quiet retirement as she enters her ninth decade? As if. "You only have one life," she's reminded us. "You might as well be interesting."

INSTRUCTIONS

To use, carefully press out the doll and cross-piece and assemble the stand as shown below.

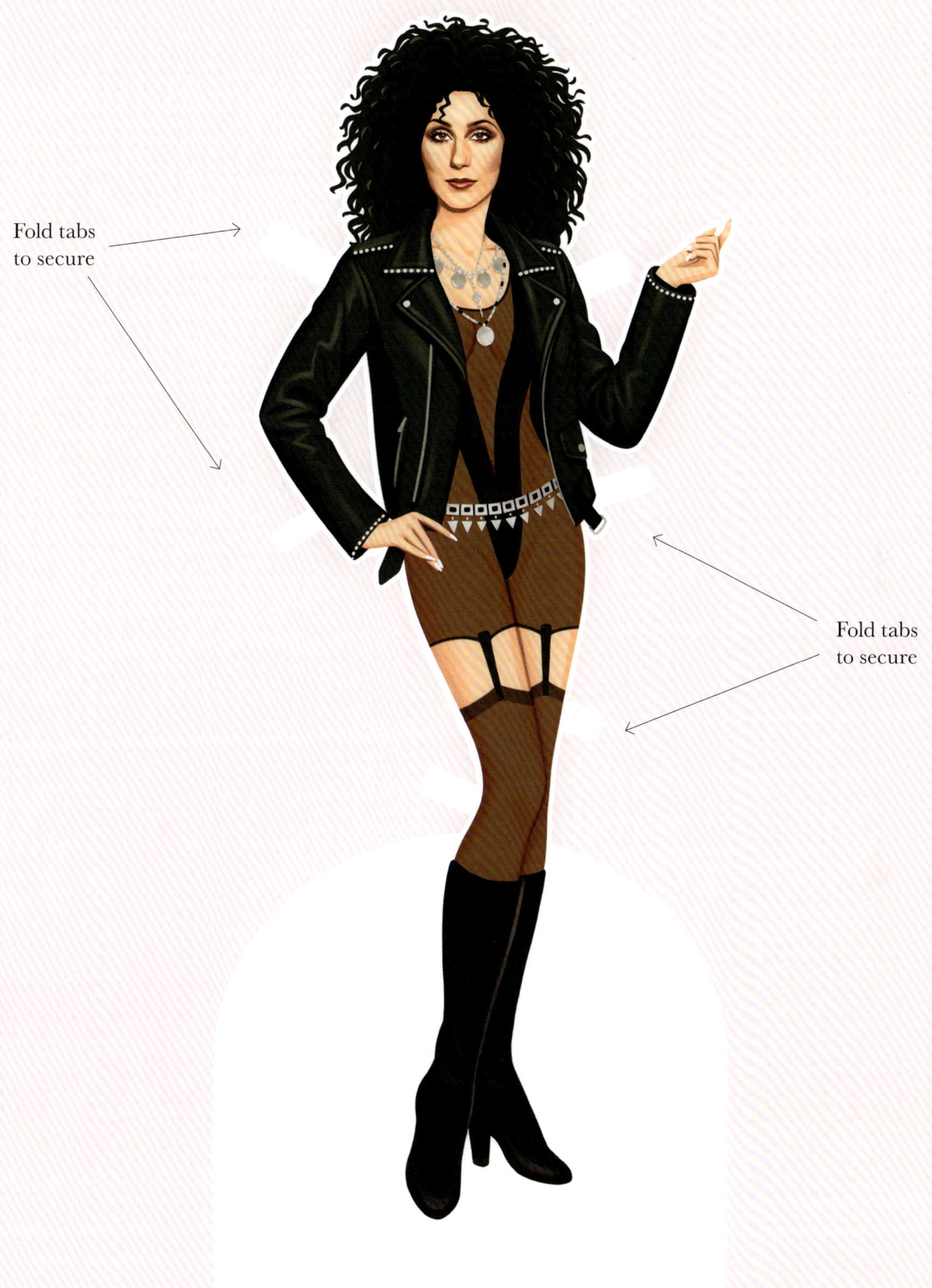

Press out the outfits and get dressing.
Style Cher in her iconic looks, or mix and match
to create something brand new.

30th GOLDEN GLOBE AWARDS

The Sonny & Cher Comedy Hour began in 1971, as much out of desperation as reinvention. The pair had ridden a rocket of success, only to find it crashing back to earth. They had their first big hit in 1965, with "I Got You Babe," but eventually audiences tailed off and they needed a new hook. So they started playing small nightclub gigs that showcased songs, stories, and jokes.

When a CBS executive saw the act, he offered Sonny and Cher a six-week variety slot to fill a seasonal hole in their broadcast TV schedule. The concept was pretty simple: they would introduce each episode, banter and sing a little, and then amuse each other – and hopefully viewers – with a range of broad sketches featuring stars like Carol Burnett and unknowns including Teri Garr and Steve Martin.

The show was meant to be a quickie replacement, a throwaway stopgap for slow summer months. But thanks to Cher's charismatic talent, the pair's odd-couple chemistry, and Bob Mackie's scandalously skin-baring outfits, it was an instant hit.

Because the network had a rule against visible navels on women, censors would arrive to her fittings with rulers. She and Mackie nodded, agreed, and then did what they wanted, figuring – correctly – that no one could argue with ratings.

It wasn't much of a surprise when *The Sonny & Cher Comedy Hour* earned a Golden Globe nomination for Best Musical or Comedy Series in 1973. Decades later, Cher still fondly remembers the night for two reasons: First, she was proud to be nominated at the same ceremony where one of her favorite films, *The Godfather*, was honored. And second, she loved Mackie's sequined and psychedelic keyhole crop top and flared pants, which she topped with a giant fox-fur, monogrammed coat (that she later wished she hadn't worn: "Times were different then," she acknowledged).

She and Sonny lost to *All in the Family*, but her outré look managed to grab the spotlight anyway, "with my belly button once again the focus of attention."

45th ACADEMY AWARDS

Cher's first dramatic big-screen performance, in the 1969 indie *Chastity*, was an unlikely harbinger of any Oscars appearance. Written and produced by Sonny, it starred Cher as a troubled and nomadic hippie and could, charitably, be described as a bust. (The theme was, in Sonny's unfortunate recollection, "the independence women have acquired but don't necessarily want.")

Though Cher's sensitive turn generated the most positive notes in a parade of negative reviews, the overall reception had her wondering if she should ever appear in another film again. So she was delighted when the Academy invited the couple to present the award for Best Original Song. (The winner was "The Morning After," from *The Poseidon Adventure*.)

This was the first year the Academy Awards were televised internationally, making it a major media opportunity for the pair and their show. Cher has called Mackie's jewel-encrusted, two-piece mesh design, with its dramatic, draping sleeves, "still one of my all-time favorite outfits," and her confidence was evident in the easy onstage repartee with Sonny. She complained that he never took her out, because she had nothing to wear. He looked her up and down and responded, to the delight of audiences around the world, "And you're wearing it."

1973

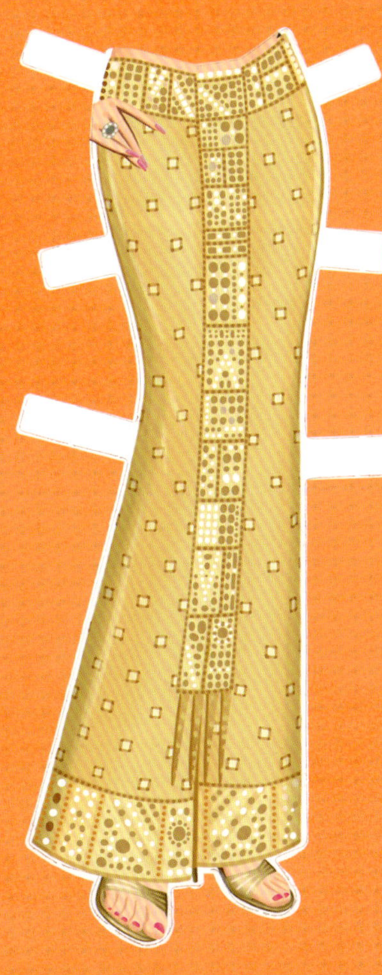

THE *Sonny & Cher* COMEDY HOUR

The couple's matching red costumes for their 1974 Valentine's Day special – particularly Cher's sequin heart-studded, tie-front cropped blouse and sparkling sequin pants – were the very picture of irony. Designed in alliance with Mackie and wardrobe head Ret Turner, this was a carefully crafted message to the world: despite growing media gossip, all was well between everyone's favorite glam duo.

As further proof, they opened the February 13th show with a warm cover of Anne Murray's song "What About Me?" Cher has said that whatever was happening offstage, the two were always united onscreen. And you can see that in this episode, where Sonny's hand is clasped around her waist, and she sings back to him with love. But their most recent record – 1973's *Mama Was a Rock and Roll Singer, Papa Used to Write All Her Songs*, had already hinted at the ongoing power struggle behind the scenes.

Indeed, while Sonny and Cher were cracking audiences up weekly on their eponymous series, they were fighting nonstop at home. Later that month, Sonny filed for divorce, and the show was cancelled for good.

1974

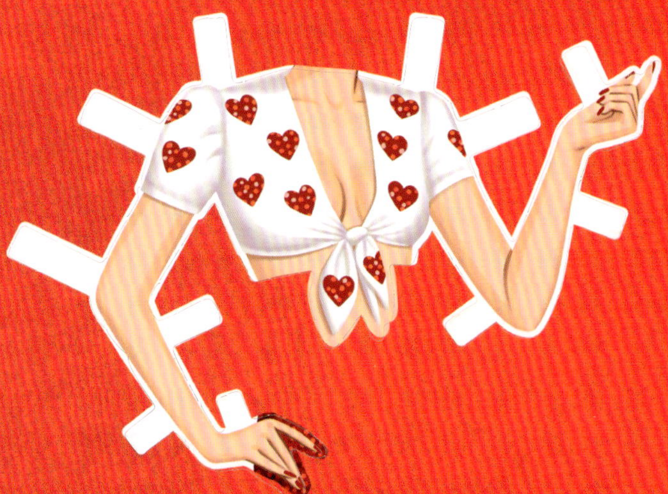

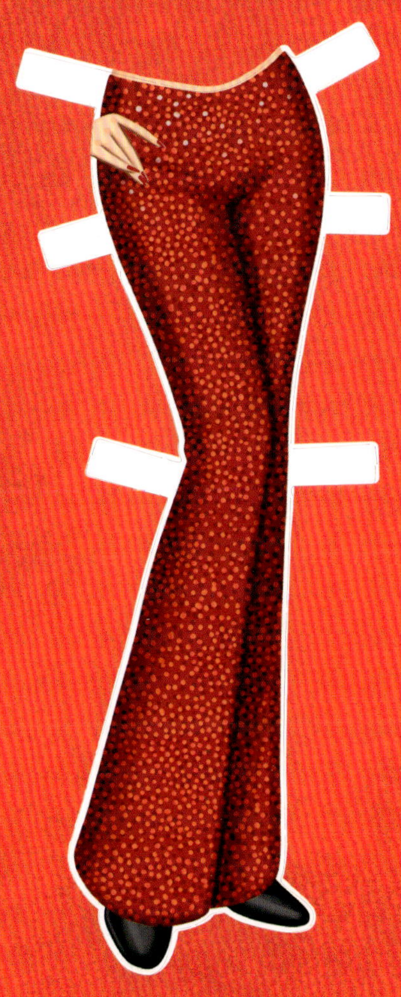

HAPPY
Valentine's
DAY
FROM THE
SONNY & CHER
SHOW
XX

1974 MET GALA

The Met Gala hasn't always captured worldwide attention the way it does today. In fact, Cher's 1974 appearance is credited with helping transform the event into the celebrity-driven spectacle it has since become.

Both she and Mackie knew that all eyes would be on her that night. She had just split from Sonny, which led to the end of their beloved show and professional partnership. Also, it was widely reported that one of the reasons she'd left was because she felt Sonny was too controlling. Cher's arrival on the red carpet was undeniably an announcement that she was her own woman, unafraid to take risks. And this "nude dress" – which Mackie sprayed with water so it would cling to her body as she walked in – was nothing if not risky.

The gown was made of sheer souffle fabric (which turned out to be so flammable it was later banned in the USA), embellished with crystal beading and cascading feathers. All that exquisite detail still left little to the imagination, which caused a huge uproar. One reporter bluntly asked Cher if she felt "naked at the Met." "I feel just fine," she responded, with the unflappable poise of a natural-born disrupter.

A few months later she wore the provocative dress again on the cover of *Time* magazine, which sold out in some US states and was banned in others. When Kim Kardashian wore a similarly sheer Roberto Cavalli gown to the Met Gala in 2015, she proudly credited Cher as her inspiration. The homage was clear – not just to the style, but to the trailblazing woman who wore it first.

1974

Harry Langdon PHOTO SESSION

By 1978, Cher had been through it. Her relationship with Southern rocker Gregg Allman was a years-long rollercoaster, covered in exhaustive detail by the press and followed with equal fervor by fans and detractors alike.

The unlikely couple married in 1975 – three days after she finalized her divorce from Sonny – split about a week later, reconciled and had son Elijah Blue in 1976, and released a critically and commercially derided album as Allman and Woman in 1977. Soon they were living separate lives: Cher started dating KISS frontman Gene Simmons even as her divorce from Allman dragged on.

Meanwhile, she and Sonny reunited for a new show in 1976, but audiences were uncomfortable with their divorce and the series was cancelled the next year. She also released two solo albums during this period, both of which flopped.

On the flip side, the 1976 Mego Cher Fashion Doll – outfitted by Bob Mackie, natch – outsold all others that year, including Barbie. And her 1978 television show, *Cher… Special*, was both a ratings success and an Emmy winner.

In retrospect, the late 1970s were a period of transition for Cher – a bridge between the years in which she was so often defined by the men in her life, and the big things that were coming.

While plotting her own renewal, there was no better way for Cher to hint at her imminent reinvention than to don another bold look. For a photoshoot with celebrity photographer Harry Langdon, Mackie's electric-blue spandex catsuit with diamante accents and silver knee-high pirate boots told the world they hadn't seen the last of Cher.

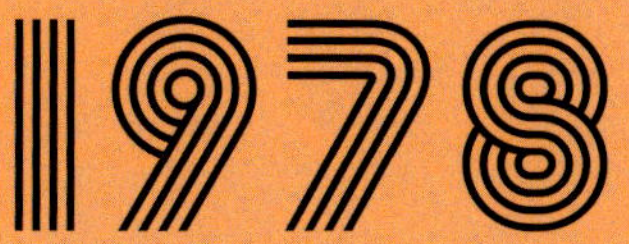
1978

Take Me Home ALBUM COVER

By 1979, Cher had already released fourteen studio albums to wildly varying success. She was a single mom to Elijah Blue and Chaz. She'd endured multiple personal scandals. And it had all happened as visibly as possible.

But if anyone knew how to shift their public image *and* ride a tide, it was Cherilyn Sarkisian LaPiere Bono Allman. After years of being famously attached, she was ready to make a statement: she was newly single – and newly independent. She dropped all her surnames and – legally at least – became "just" Cher.

Her album *Take Me Home* announced the transformation loud and clear. Gone was the TV-friendly boho hippie. In her place stood an overtly sexual, unapologetic – though, let's be honest, still enthusiastically camp – disco-era Cher.

The album became her first to go gold since 1973's *Half-Breed*, and it's fair to say that at least a little of that success was thanks to the cover – a Mackie-designed warrior fantasy she once described as "barmaid from Valhalla." With a floor-length pleated cape, winged bikini, cuffs and headdress, knee-high boots, and a suitably dramatic scabbard attached at the hip, this all-gold ensemble represents Mackie and Cher at their most camp. And actual Vikings also wore sexy gold bikinis, knee-high boots, and winged headpieces … right?

1979

58th ACADEMY AWARDS

Who would dream of wearing this, shall we say, atypical attire to Hollywood's most formal event? There's only one conceivable answer. And when you learn the reason, you'll love her more.

In the 1985 movie *Mask*, Cher stars as Rusty Dennis, mother to Rocky (played by Eric Stoltz), who is disfigured by craniodiaphyseal dysplasia. Her performance is a tour-de-force – fierce, cool, and absolutely stunning to those who had no idea she could act.

She won the Best Actress award at Cannes – not an easy crowd to impress – and was nominated for a Golden Globe. But you know what she didn't get? The Oscar nod everyone assumed was coming next. The rumor was that she was too inexperienced – and, well, too vulgar – to be considered Best Actress material. (The award eventually went to eight-time nominee Geraldine Page for the period drama *The Trip to Bountiful*.)

Instead, Cher was invited to present the Oscar for Best Supporting Actor – a gesture that felt like a patronizing consolation prize. So she and Mackie decided that if the Academy was too small-minded to accept her on her terms, they would respond the best way they knew how.

She didn't have to utter a single word to get her message across loud and clear. The morning after she arrived in this midriff-baring, showgirl-inspired crop top, skirt, cape, and cuff get-up – topped with a towering, feathered headdress, because of course – all anyone could talk about was Cher.

Legend.

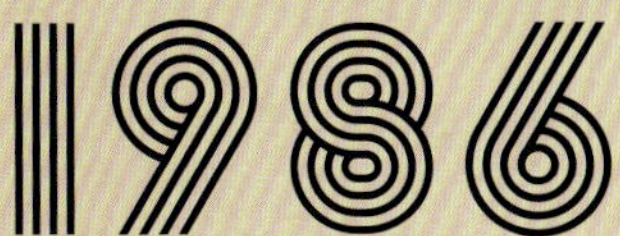
1986

MOONSTRUCK

Welcome to another upswing on the wild ride that is Cher's life. She had tried to be a movie star back in 1969, but *Chastity* was so poorly received that she felt too insecure to revisit the idea. Then, in 1982, Robert Altman cast her in *Come Back to the 5 and Dime Jimmy Dean, Jimmy Dean.* This was followed by powerhouse performances in *Silkwood*, *Mask*, *The Witches of Eastwick*, and *Suspect*. But – despite a nomination for *Silkwood* – still no Oscar.

Then came *Moonstruck*.

Perhaps no role was better suited to Cher than Loretta Castorini, a wryly intelligent bookkeeper who still lives at home with her parents. Though indifferently engaged to her dopey boyfriend (Danny Aiello), she's never really known true love … until she meets his volatile brother, Ronny (Nicolas Cage).

The stubbornly practical Loretta typically wears muted sweaters and shapeless skirts. But when Ronny invites her to see *La Bohème* at the Met, she impulsively buys a gorgeous red velvet and silk dress. This gown was designed by Oscar-winning costumer Theoni V. Aldredge to reflect Loretta's emotional transformation – and Ronny falls in love the moment he sees her in it.

By the way, if you remember the dress being blue, you're (sort of) right. The color was changed for the iconic poster image of Cher celebrating against an azure sky. But in the film, it's the rich red that makes Ronny – and the audience – catch their breath. ("Wow. Thank you," he says with quiet wonder when he removes her Calvin Klein coat and sees her in this strapless number, newly styled curls skimming her shoulders.)

Funny, earthy, and romantic, *Moonstruck* was one of the biggest hits of 1987… and Cher finally went home with a well-earned award on Oscar night.

1987

IF I COULD *Turn* BACK TIME

By 1989, Cher was a veteran performer, an accomplished actress, and forty-three years old. No longer merely a pop star, but a multihyphenate icon.

But if we've learned anything by now, it's that nobody tells Cher what to do. And that she has no patience for sexist societal strictures.

Instead of softening her image, Cher doubled down, daring anyone to tell her how to be a woman. She was perfectly in control when the video for her soon-to-be-smash single, "If I Could Turn Back Time," hit MTV (then the main medium for building buzz).

Everyone watched in shock – or awe, depending on their perspective – as she strutted across a US Navy battleship, surrounded by wildly cheering sailors and indisputably phallic cannons. Have we mentioned what she was wearing? Garters. High-heeled boots. A leather jacket. And the head-turning "seat belt" look, specially designed by Mackie using a sheer bodystocking and two strips of fabric, to show off her, er, rear-admiral tattoos.

The moral outrage hit a fever pitch. The Navy issued a stern statement disavowing their participation and MTV refused to air the video during daylight hours.

And the album, *Heart of Stone*, went triple platinum.

Today, it doesn't feel remotely controversial to see a mid-career artist brazenly claiming her power. And you know exactly who we should be thanking for that.

Despite both Cher and Mackie admitting to being a little suprised (and perhaps embarrassed) by their own gall, it is undoubtedly one of Cher's most iconic looks and she has continued to wear versions of it in the years since.

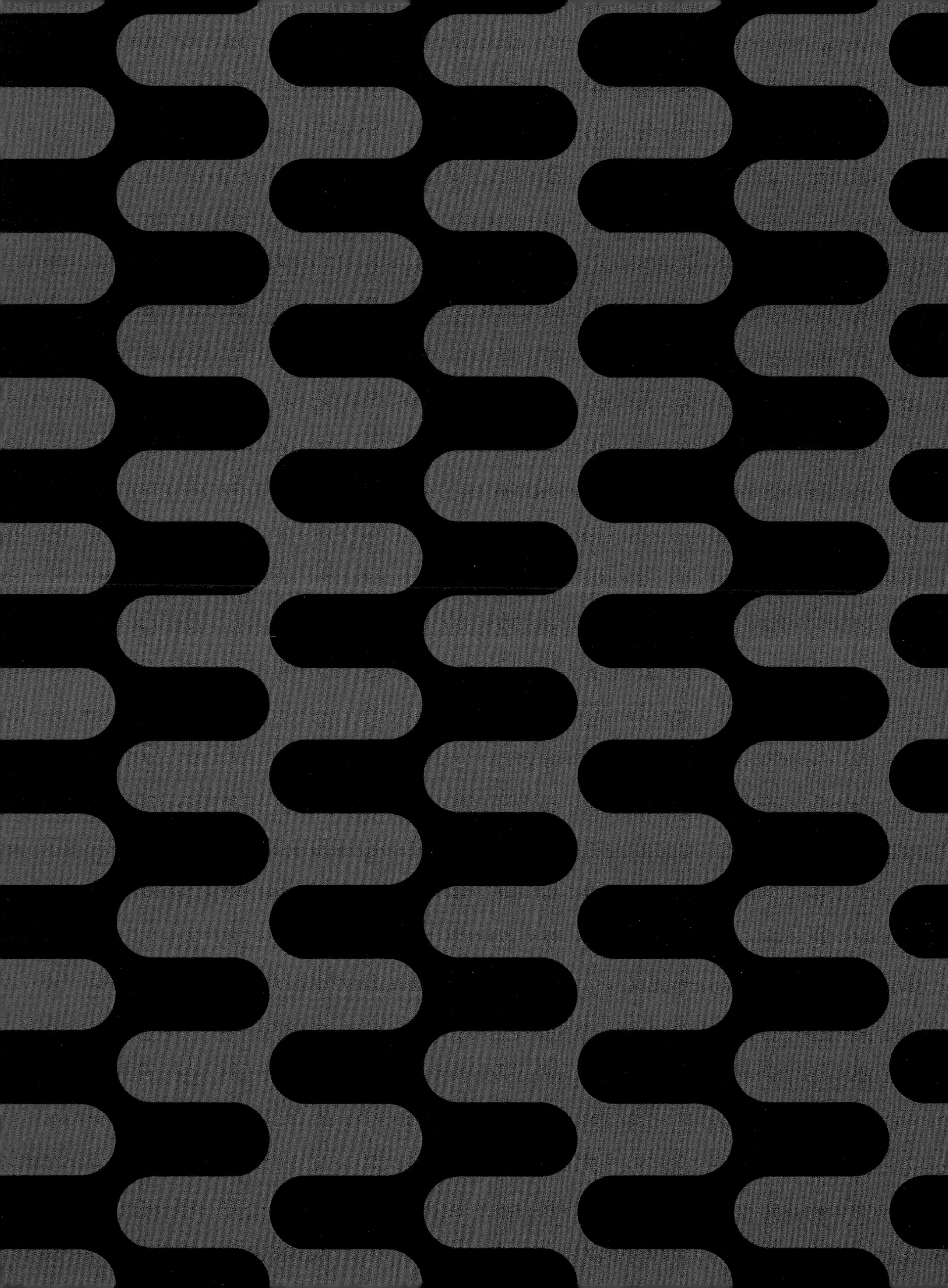

1989

Carol Burnett: 90 YEARS OF LAUGHTER + LOVE

Back in 1967, when Cher and Sonny were invited onto *The Carol Burnett Show* it was a huge coup for the young artists. Carol introduced them as "leaders of the new wild, way-out movement," but that wasn't the most memorable moment.

Before the taping, Cher was told that Burnett's costume designer would be fitting her for a special dress. Who walked in? The great Bob Mackie. "What I didn't know," she said later, "was that he would become, hands down, one of the most important men in my life."

That wasn't an exaggeration. They have collaborated for decades, not only on outfits but on her public image. When you think of Cher – for that matter, when you turn the pages of this book – you nearly always see Mackie.

So, of course he designed the ensemble she wore to honor her great friend Carol Burnett in 2023. The ethereal gold gown was originally created for Cher's Las Vegas residency, but what makes it special in this context is the full-circle symbolism. This outfit is nothing less than a tribute to the legacy of a partnership that began all those years ago.

The "Goddess of Pop" look recalls many of Mackie's signature outfits made famous by his greatest muse: illusion fabrics, hand-sewn beading, sequins, sequins, and more sequins, and uniquely extravagant headpieces. This one-of-a-kind halo, in particular, alludes to her incomparable status as an angel in Mackie's own life.

2023

HAPPY
Valentine's
DAY
FROM THE
SONNY & CHER
SHOW

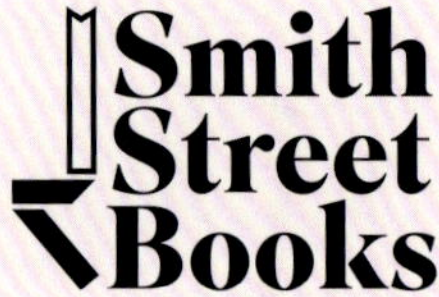

Published in 2026 by Smith Street Books
Naarm (Melbourne) | Australia
smithstreetbooks.com

Distributed outside of ANZ, North & Latin America by
Thames & Hudson Ltd., 6–24 Britannia Street, London, WC1X 9JD
thamesandhudson.com

EU Authorised Representative: Interart S.A.R.L.
19 rue Charles Auray, 93500 Pantin, Paris, France
productsafety@thameshudson.co.uk; www.interart.fr

ISBN: 978-1-9232-3985-2

Smith Street Books respectfully acknowledges the Wurundjeri People of the Kulin Nation, who are the Traditional Owners of the land on which we work, and we pay our respects to their Elders past and present.

Publisher: Hannah Koelmeyer
Project editor: Lucy Grant
Illustrator: Helen Green
Design & layout: Susan Le
Text: Elizabeth Weitzman
Text editor: Lorna Hendry
Proofreader: Cressida McDermott
Prepress: Megan Ellis
Production manager: Aisling Coughlan

Printed & bound in China by C&C Offset Printing Co., Ltd.

Book 438
10 9 8 7 6 5 4 3 2 1